Poems
from my heart

by CHELSEY FLAUNA

Order this book online at www.trafford.com
or email orders@trafford.com

Most Trafford titles are also available at major online book retailers.

Printed in the United States of America.

ISBN: 978-1-4269-6560-9

Library of Congress Control Number: 2011905984

Trafford rev. 04/13/2011

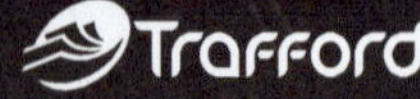

www.trafford.com

North America & international
toll-free: 1 888 232 4444 (USA & Canada)
phone: 250 383 6864 fax: 812 355 4082

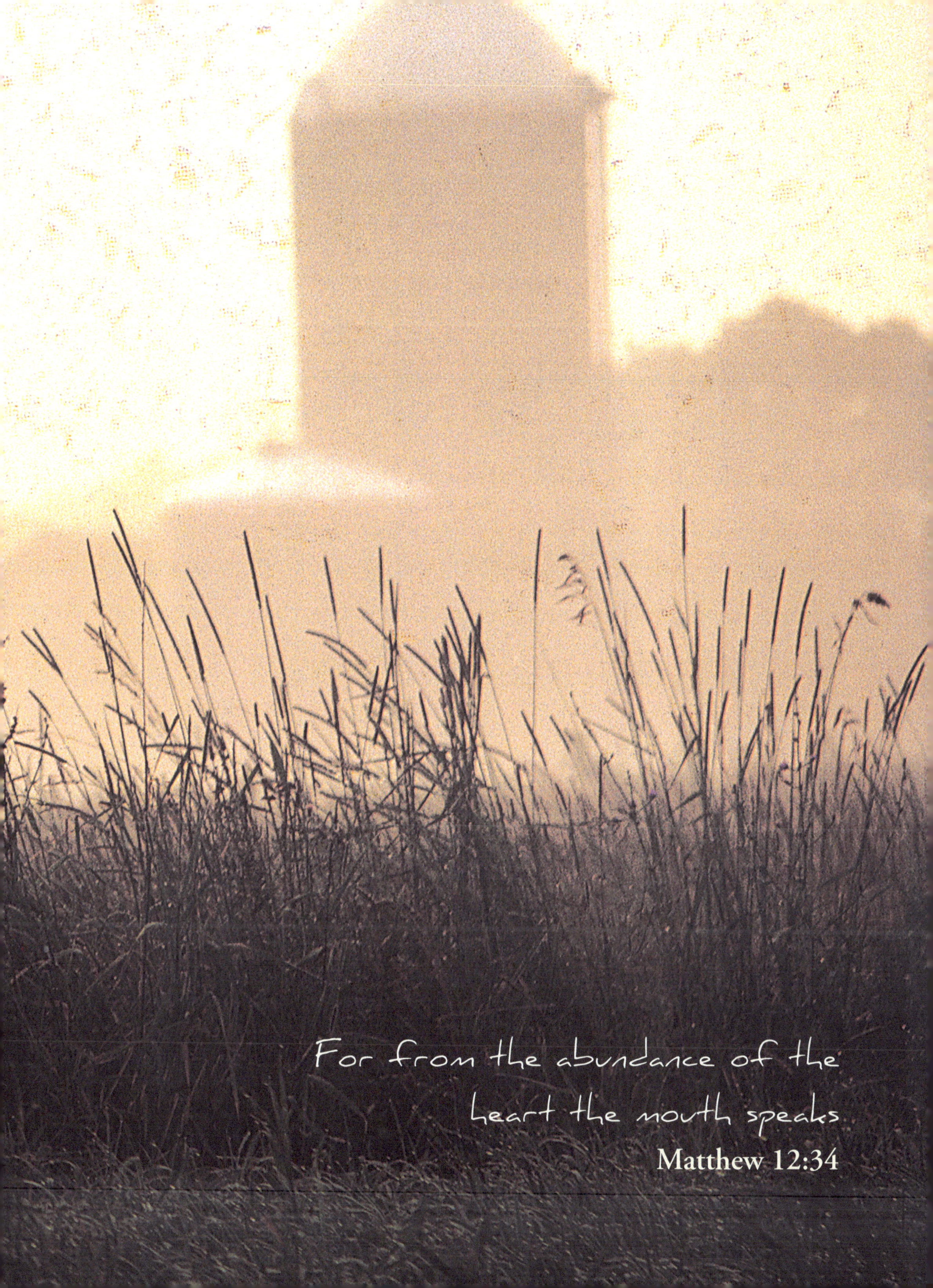

For from the abundance of the
heart the mouth speaks
Matthew 12:34

A Simple Word of Thanks

By Chelsey Flauna

Of all the sinful, grievous things

The worst by far is to never say

A simple word of "Thanks".

Therefore, dear Lord, thank you,

Thank you, for land, and sea, and air;

Thank you for all those who care.

A FLOWER'S PASSING

Tis words of comfort I speak, dear ones...,
At your flower's passing. I pray your hearts may
Find its ease in the comfort now I am bringing.
Oh, truly know where flowers go, tis Eternal Spring,
An Everlasting Garden of Joy.
For under the Savior's brightful gaze
They laugh and sing, play and dance
Thru' all eternal days
Angelic beings in gleaming array sing
Melodious songs, while playing upon golden harps
As lil cherubs and flowers play "ring a rosy"
Most merrily.
When your sweet flower entered thru'
The Glorious Garden gates,
She met my lil rose, and playmates
Forever they became....
In golden bowls before The Throne,
Our tears, like our prayers, most precious
Glowing orbs, are kept until that
"Day of Days"
When Jesus wipes every tear away...

Chelsey Flauna

HAPPY LIL CLOWN

By Chelsey Flauna

Happy lil clown, jolly, jolly jump around,
Laugh and play with me !
Tho' sometimes I get sad, then you turn
Around, my lil clown, and kiss my tears
Away.
But happy lil clown, when you're feeling down,
Who wipes your tears away ?

Oh, Don't You Know

By Chelsey Flauna

At times, you take my hand and you speak my name as
As we say, "Hello".
Then, with tearful eyes I watch you go.
Beloved, oh, don't you know? I love you so.
But always, always you turn and go!
Beloved, oh don't you know?
The one for whom you turn to, will never,
Ever love you ! But yet you go !
My beloved, I love you so ! Yet someday I know,
I'll have your hand, and you'll never go.
Tho' when you've turned and I've watch you go.
Still, still I love you so

Young Doves Too Soon Gone

By Chelsey Flauna

They stood before my shop, like many times before,
Their noses 'gainst the windowed frost,
There were warm exchanges
In our eyes, and across our faces, Grandmama,
Was with "her", my dearest heart, "her" that was
To me, the promised spring of wonders more to come.
Then came the Nazi horde marching in uniform…!
Grandmama made silent protest with her eyes as they
Passed.
Then my love, my sweet dove was bound and taken!
Taken amidst the jeers and howls of the gathering crowds.
Grandmama, in an effort to halt them, raised her cane,
Saying,"Oh no, don't!" "Oh no, never no, no, no!"
But with singleness and ease of movement, they sent
The old woman through the half-frozen glass, she laid
Bruised and bleeding amongst the shattered shards
Of window pane, her final words of "Take me instead!"
Seeped from her with an agonized quiet sigh.
I too was then bound and taken! And, my shop was
All but rubble from the looting, howling mob.
And.. the falling first snows of winter were stained
With the blood of young doves, too soon gone

In memory of those
That perished in the
Holocaust

LIFE LEAVES

Oh, how delicate, how sweetly fragrant,
The dewy blossoms, and how lush, and green
The spring leaves upon the branches.
The summer is warm and joyous with
The merry voices of children at play, while
The little birds hop about, trying their new
Wings, as the bees about the blossoms so busy.
Soon will come fruit, heavy and full sweet
Upon the branches.
But with the flush of autumn, the blossoms
Are withered and now gone away. As with the
Leaves turning soft yellow, crimson, gold, and
Scarlet upon the branches. At times, for some,
The killing frost comes early, then comes no fruit
With the summer.
The winter winds chill cold down even to
Roots, and the leaves are now withered brown
And driven to the ground. Then they are gathered
Up and heaped to burn upon the "Rubbish pile".
No longer do the children come to play. "For
Its far to cold to play out-of-doors, on such a
Wintry day." Says mother.
But, oh how melancholy tho' to think
I shan't see them come spring. Tis better
Now to remember them and the little birds,
Playing, as the snow lies deeply around me.

(Because Life leaves, for Life ne'er
Intended to ere remain.
Life comes only to pass away.
So, we must, this day, choose
Where we shall be gathered,
And there forever stay.)

By Chelsey Flauna

SOFTLY COMES MORNING

By Chelsey Flauna

The blue-gray mist whiffs through
The dark night still within the
Trees…softly
And… I wish I were in
Love
The dawn tips the leaves upon
The nearby trees golden, as the
Night flies away…softly
And…I wish I were in
Love
The young birds dart the sky
Fresh from the Spring that has
Since passed "Good-bye . . .!"
For autumn is here now and
Their wings they do try…softly
And…I wish I were in
Love
For Love heats the heart, warming
The blood, as it sparks the eyes and
Plays a song anew upon lovers
Lips … so softly
Oh, how I wish I were in
Love

Nature At Twilight

By Chelsey Flauna

How lovely the living elements
Shimmering across the broad
Expansive sky.
There glistening between the
Horizons, in the brilliant afternoon
Radiance.
The Earth breathes, pulsating
Rushing, pushing upon the misty
Fleeces, what feathered graces
Saunter miles above me .
But ah, what creatures, I have
Spied aloft !
Sunset red roaring dragons,
Sensuous fishes, and winged
Horses. With the billowing sails
Of Spanish galleons soaring
Thru' clouds of ghostly seas

OWNERSHIP

By Chelsey Flauna

The Lord God Almighty, seated
Upon Heaven's throne, says "Mine,"
O'er all existence, and very rightly so.
For what is there in existence, that,
He has not made so? From the brilliant sun,
To the shimmering stars, o'er all the golden
Sunrises, to the flaming sunsets of eventide, of
The creatures that grace the blue above, and fills the
Trees with song, to the monsters of the "Deep"
That bitter sweetly sings and roams the oceans
Beneath.
It was He that made them so.

Mortal man says "Mine", in ignorant, errant, folly.
For, indeed, Mortal man owns nothing, not Time, nor
Place, or even gold, but especially not "The Soul."
Yes, "The Breath Of Life" is housed within
That God to Man be gifted.
Yet at Its departure, the mortal self goes back to
Soil again." The Soul", then to its owner departs,
Be it Heaven, or it be Hell.

Hell says "Mine"(And sadly so), by "Right Of Conquest",
As that, of predator and prey, over every captured soul,
For, remember well, He, "The Father of Liars", is a
"Ravening lion", seeking those He can devour!
To torment, eternally so, in defiant, lusting, rage!

But what of the redemption that Jesus' death
Made so for one and all? Even for those poor,
Wretched souls, now in captivity, eternally!
That all their lives, they neglected and ignored,
And, thus refused!
They are now, forever to reproachfully regret,
And to suffer, and to suffer, and to suffer, and to suffer!

THE COST OF LOVE

By Chelsey Flauna

Love hurts, oh not in Heaven,
But on Earth.
Mirth and joy come at such
Cost ! Pain and sorrow, tears of
Loss, tis of such doth love cost .

The value of Spring the old
Trees know,
From scorching Summers,
And Winter's cold.

Twas after it had broken,
Did the Tin man
Truly know he, indeed,
Possessed a heart, a soul !

Twas only after The Christ
Was Crucified,
Have some begun to
Comprehend His significances

The Power
Of
Grace

Throughout the span of our
Mortal History, from our feeble first
Attempts, to the point where we
Cry out, in having reached our limits .
There is the power of "God's Grace"
Abounding by reason of the cross .
So that His own in confidence most
Abundant have declared throughout
Time and history,
Yes, we are weak, but He is strong !
Yes, we can do all things, through
Christ who strengthens us !

By Chelsey Flauna

Three Lil Roses

It's been said that "Children
are roses from God's own garden."
Now a single rose is gracious and sweet.
Two little roses are twice as neat!
But three little roses truly means
A hand picked blessing from God, indeed!

By Chelsey Flauna

On This Night

Behold . . .
His star that shines the brightest !
Listen to what the shepherds tell.

Above a lowly stable outside Bethlehem
Glorious Angelic hosts sing
Of the Newborn King.

Come light the torches follow me . . ..
Lo wise men from the East
Bearing gifts fit only for kings
.

Now ring the bells, blow loud your horns
Sing in joy, to all the world tell
Shout praises to our Newborn King !
For on this night, the Christ is come !

Chelsey Flauna

Window Scene

By Chelsey Flauna

With easy grace, I watch, as the pattern'd shadows
Of curtain lace, waltz across my bedroom walls.
As the day slowly advances, I smile pleasantly at
The shadow'd lace, swaying to its "Day Song",
With the fragrant afternoon breezes.
Perched upon my windowsill, kitten dreamily
Watches the hummingbirds feast upon the latticework
Of honeysuckle out upon the garden wall.
But now, with day ending, Evening gently begins enfolding
One and all with its inky curtains.
The pattern'd shadows of lace, now blows a kiss,
And waves a sweet adieu.
Kitten, rouses from her perch upon the sill, and leaps
Down upon my bed, (the hummingbirds are done and gone),
She busily washes her face, tidies her fur, and purrs
Warmly to me. Briefly I stand gazing out my window with her.
As Evening draws Night's curtains to its final close.
And....
We, that dwell unseen herein, (kitten and I) stand briefly,
Gazing out into the serene, and starry, moonlit sky.

A MOON-LIT STROLL

By Chelsey Flauna

The evening was pleasant and warm to me,
As the soft summer breezes stirred,
The scent of night-blooming jasmine,
Orange blossoms, and honeysuckle,
Throughout the garden, and the surrounding
Grounds with such fragrant delight .

I stood gazing up into the starry sky.
O' how like Tiffany diamonds the stars,
Studded against the blue-black drape of
Night !

How I love strolling about as I wait . . . .
Wait for him, I promised .Yes I promised
To wait in the garden, by the latticework
Of blossoms along the garden wall .

From a silvery half-moon, all was bathed
In the soft glow of moonlight . The garden
Glistened from the dew giving a gentle
Gleam to everything .

Tender thoughts of him, cause a bittersweet
Smile to appear, then slowly tears stream
Down . . ."Why, oh why, did daddy disapprove
So ? " " For truly I love him so dearly ."

"But tonight, tonight he'll come for me !"
"Then we'll go and be wed, and live happily
Forever more !"
"Oh, my dear-heart, hurry, hurry to me !"
As I stroll in the moonlight . . .waiting, waiting !

"Hey, look at you, man !" "You look like ya
Just saw a ghost !" "I . . .uh did . . . I think !"
" To catch up with you guys, I hopped the fence
Of that ole' place, and ran through the garden."
"Then I saw this girl . . .kind of pretty, but
Dressed in old-time clothes ."
" She was standing there, holding this kitten,
In her arms ." " She looked sorta sad to me ."
" Hey , ya know, I've heard tales, of
That place being haunted !"
" But I did see a girl in old time clothes,
With a kitten in her arms, too !"
" Aw, come on man, enough, let's go
Home !"
In the moonlight, I stroll through the
Garden, waiting for him, by the
Latticework of blossoms, I promised . . .
Even forever .

WINTRY MORN

The cold soft gray light of dawn,
With its fleecy light blue-gray,
Blanket of clouds, whispers to me
Upon the breeze, that winter is come.
So where, my love, now are you?
Once, twas true, I felt Winter warm
Upon me, that now finds me chilled,
To my very heart, my soul!
The autumn gold and scarlet,
That once was upon the leaves,
Are now faded brown, and withered,
Fluttering down upon the ground in
They're dying.
Oh, but where are you, my dear-heart?
Come before the last embers, that once
Flamed so, indeed, it made winter
Warm, and I glowed with love and joy!
Oh, come now, that our embers be not
Extinguished, possibly, forever!
Come; make this wintry morn, flame-up,
Warm once more for me! For how I wish to
Glow again with love and joy!

- Chelsey Flauna -

On The Road to Wisdom

I walked awhile with
Happiness
What a lovely walk, and a pleasant talk,
Was had by one and all
Though, afterwards, I pondered what it was
That I had learned . . .
Then I walked awhile
With Sorrow
What a lonely dreadful walk, and tearful talk
Had we along the way
Though, afterwards, I realized
What alot I learned. . .

– Chelsey Flauna –

OF WISDOM AND FOLLY

My beloved son,
Make "Wisdom" your most treasured friend.
For indeed, truly she is, and abide with her forever.
And, drink most heartily the drafts of "TRUTH"
From "Wisdom's" golden cup!
Then, you shall be free from folly,
With Its much regret, and bitter reproof.
For those that ignore, dear "WISDOM",
Those that refuse to follow her,
Or search out "The TRUTH".
Tis, by their own willful folly,
That they're condemned already,
To fall prey to lies.
And....the more preposterous,
The more they're adherent to .

By Chelsey Flauna

MY WORDS OF "SELAH"

Remember me, my dear loved ones,
When gazing down a hallway, looking
Out a sunlit window, with summertime
Streaming in, through the open curtain lace
Or when…spring arrives, do lay down in
A grassy meadow, breathe in the sweet
Green grass, the flowers, the warmth of
The musky earth, and kindly,
Remember me.

Then stroll the seashore, that I love so, listening
To the waves, crashing and roaring, to and fro.
All around the sad songs of the shorebirds' calls,
Filling the salty air. Then note please, how fair blue
The sky is o'er the ocean wide. And kindly,
Remember me.

There, please send my ashes to the windy sea,
Letting it scatter, far and wide, my remains,
To the sea, the ever moving, restless, shimmering
Sea
Then "Selah" (meaning to pause and think deeply)
These words of mine, and kindly,
Remember me.

For at the end of all that mankind is, Jesus is there.
He is above and beyond, all that we ever do !
For as with the disciples, having fished throughout
The day and long into the night, to no avail at sunrise,
Jesus then fills their nets to over flowing,
And, not for the first time !

Jesus is there at the end of all we ever feel or fear.
In the midst of sorrow and despair, Jesus is there !
At Life's start, all along our way, and when we've come to " the end" !
He's above and beyond; all that mankind can do or say,
More than the parents that raise us, or the doctors that
Birth, and maintain us, the teachers that educate us,
And the preachers that minister to us,
Jesus is there !
For back to fishing the disciples went, in broken-hearted anguish
And despair
Their hopes dashed at Christ's Crucifixion.
But Jesus was there, upon the shore, a blazing fire to warm
Them, and food cooking upon the flames, and yes, Jesus alive !
And speaking words of understanding and comfort, and resolve,
(Especially for Peter) !
Thus, at the time of your pain, sorrow, fear or grief, Jesus is there!
With the fire of the Holy Spirit to warm and comfort, His Holy Word
To feast your soul upon, and nourish you, and Himself, within to speak
Understanding to your heart. SELAH!

Chelsey Flauna

Someday...

By Chelsey Flauna

Someday...
He who made us,
Will in triumph return, and make all
Things right and new.

Someday..
The strong will not victimize the meek,
For there will be understanding.

Someday..
The only tears that's shed, will be those
Of "Great Joy".

Someday
The true measure of a man will be in his
Ability to love, and be loved
.

Someday...
Righteousness will have reigned so long,
That nothing else is remembered.

Someday...
There will be justice,
For He who made us,
Will have lead captivity captive.

But this is...Someday
For now we suffer like a woman in travail,
Awaiting the "Promise of the Hope", fulfilled.

My Bridget

Autumn bright,
My Bridget
Amber and cream her
Silky coat
With piercing eyes of
Liquid golden jade
She warms my heart,
Purring in motherly
Fashion at her station
Under my lil one's cot
For night after night,
I find my kitty cat
guarding her sleeping
Curly-headed bundle

In fondest memory,
Of my cat Bridget
For she cared for my son as her own
February 14, 1988 - July 26, 2001

Little Bird
(In a Winter Scene)
By Chelsey Flauna

Little Bird, winging through the chilly mid-day sky;
You, soaring high through a stark and icy sky
Did you know I watch you with jealous eyes?
For as a child, I once wished I could fly.
I watch you little one, lightly touch down,
Down, among the branches of that picturesque old oak;
Its being fills the backdrop in my lil winter scene.
I sit gazing out my window, watching while you sing.

THE LIL BIRD REPLIES
By Chelsey Flauna

O'er trees and rooftops I
Fly.
Soaring high 'crossed billowed
Skies.
Oh poor man, that cannot fly.
Did you know, I watch you with
Curious eyes?
Oh human, the things I've seen !
I've nested in vallies green,
Where you, oh man, have never
Been.
I've sailed with the wind thru'
Many a golden morn.
Oh, 'tis a pity that Man
Can't fly.
Yet, 'tis for him the Savior died.

Sea And Shore

By Chelsey Flauna

Oh the love between
Sea and shore !
Ever touching, ever reaching,
Always caressing.
Meeting always in sweeping
Kisses, long embraces, and
Slow releases.
The sea, rushing to meet her
Eternal love.
The shore, standing, beckoning onward,
Forever, his one beloved.
While quiet moon and dazzling sun
Orchestras from up above.
Heavenly, attentive watchers
The sun, moon, and stars.
A' fore Man ever came to stand,
Gazing at sea and shore.
Oh the sweet, eternal love
Of the sea and shore.

For Timothy

by Chelsey Flauna

I didn't think He saw me
"But God sees everything" says
Grammy. "He writes it in
His "account books"
But for such a lil thing I did,
Sin is somethin' mighty weighty
And I'm not even six.
Now I'm standing in the corner,
My face all wet. I whisper,
"Gee God, I sure am sorry !".
Then He whispers back to me, "There,
There lil dear, on a hill long ago,
I want you to know, I wiped the
"account books" clean".

FOR YOU ONLY LOVE

By Chelsey Flauna

You are my youth and learning
You are sweet passions burning
You keep me forever yearning
So let our love keep
growing

In tears and health stay near me
My love, please ne'er leave me
For like the trees need rain and shine
Please understand, you'll always be
Mine, to have and to hold, forever
Together, as we grow old. . .

BLINDNESS

By Chelsey Flauna

Sight light from the soul

Blindness wind extinguishing

The light from the soul

NIGHT BREEZES

By Chelsey Flauna

I woke in the night

Branches swaying to and fro

The tune, the wind made

REDEMPTION

By Chelsey Flauna

Mankind to sin went

All Creation then was cursed

Then love mended it

NIGHTMARES

By Chelsey Flauna

When fantasy, imagining, make-believe,

The world of dreams, become your reality,

Then beware of nightmares . . . . !

IN COMFORTING AN OLE' FRIEND

By Chelsey Flauna

Upon returning home most recently,
I found my dearest friend greatly distressed,
And sobbing !
As he unraveled his woes to me, saying,
"The printed page is dead or dying, they tell me !"
" How can this be ?" he wailed to me.
So I dried his inky tears and soothed his pages,
Smooth again.
His rumpled jacket, I then retrieved, and
Tidied it afresh for him.
We, read some of Sandburg's poetry,
And he brightened up abit.
Finally over tea with, Dear Beatrix, Dickens,
And of course Miss Emily, then he was fine,
Again.

THE QUIET LIFE

By Chelsey Flauna

We live "The quiet life", (of desperation)
In a world where hearts cry and
Dreams die .
How did this become so . . .for you
And I ?
Ever so slowly . . .ever so slowly . . .

With the rush of day and bills
To pay, the eternal ticking of
The clock . Now no longer able
To hear each other's heart beat
In the day time.
We live "The quiet life" (of desperation)

GOOD BUSINESS

By Chelsey Flauna

When good men of business,

Contented themselves no longer

To do, "Good Business"

Then both men and business

Are lost . .
.
And all suffer . . .

CONFINES

By Chelsey Flauna

How tragic to have, a boundless, limitless,

Marvelous, loving God, who's expected to work within,

The limited confines, of mere human understanding,

Or our perception of reality .

PURR KITTY

By Chelsey Flauna

Today purr kitty scratched me !
Tis true purr kitty did!
Today purr kitty scratched me,`
Then she went off and hid .
Why did purr kitty scratch me ?
For it caused me such alarm !
I love my sweet purr kitty, and
Would never do her harm .
So, when purr kitty stops hiding,
Deciding to come home. I'll tell her
That I love her, and pet and hold
Her close .
For she is my purr kitty, and I'll always
Love her so .

OF WHOM SHALL I MARRY

By Chelsey Flauna

Of whom shall I marry ?
The first said he would love me,
But first some conditions I need
Meet. Just do this and that, then
He would love me.
But this is not love, not love to me ! For love
Requires only loving .

Of whom shall I marry ?
The second said he loved me,
For my pretty eyes and shining hair !
And, ah the gleam that came from there.
But in this world there are those fairer,
Having prettier eyes and shinier hair,
And ah, the gleam that comes from there !
But this is not love, not love to me ! For love requires
Only loving .

So, of whom shall I marry ?
I'll marry him that says, " I love you,
" Always will."" In spite of the times,
When angry words fly, and hot tears
Flow in the night." "Or when Age comes
Like a thief in the night, stealing our prime ."
" Yes love, in spite of anything, I'll choose to love you, always !"
Tis him, I shall marry .

www.ingramcontent.com/pod-product-compliance
Lightning Source LLC
LaVergne TN
LVHW070202110826
845147LV00002B/480
* 9 7 8 1 4 2 6 9 6 5 6 0 9 *